# MY BODY

# My Legs and Feet

By Lloyd G. Douglas

Children's Press®
A Division of Scholastic Inc.
New York / Toronto / London / Auckland / Sydney
Mexico City / New Delhi / Hong Kong
Danbury, Connecticut

Photo Credits: Cover © Lynda Richardson/Corbis; pp. 5, 21 (top left) ©Ariel Skelley/Corbis; p. 7 © LWA-Dann Tardif/Corbis; p. 9 © Stephanie Rausser/Getty Images; pp. 11, 21 (top right) © Jim Cummins/Corbis; pp.13, 21 (bottom left) © Roy Morsch/Corbis; pp. 15, 21 (bottom right) © Corbis; p. 17 © Michael Pole/Corbis; p. 19 © Richard Nowitz/Corbis
Contributing Editor: Shira Laskin
Book Design: Michael de Guzman

Library of Congress Cataloging-in-Publication Data

Douglas, Lloyd G.
  My legs and feet / by Lloyd G. Douglas.
  p. cm.—(My body)
  Includes index.
  Summary: Simple text introduces the functions of the human foot and leg,
  as well as tools that can help people who have mobility problems.
  ISBN 0-516-24064-1 (lib. bdg.)—ISBN 0-516-22130-2 (pbk.) 33614 03517 0653
  1. Leg—Juvenile literature. 2. Foot—Juvenile literature. [1. Leg.
  2. Foot. 3. Human anatomy.] I. Title. II. Series.

  QM549.D68 2003
  612'.98—dc22
                                                2003012084

1 2 3 4 5 6 7 8 9 10 R 13 12 11 10 09 08 07 06 05 04

# Contents

I have two legs.

4

Each leg has a **knee**.

My knees help my legs **bend**.

I also have two feet.

I have five toes on each foot.

I can use my foot to **kick** a ball.

11

There are **muscles** in my legs.

The muscles help my legs move.

Legs and feet work together to help us walk.

Some people cannot use their legs and feet.

They use **wheelchairs** to get from place to place.

Some people do not
have legs.

They use legs made of
**plastic** or **metal** to walk.

Legs and feet are very useful parts of our bodies.

# New Words

**bend** (**bend**) to change the shape of something so it is no longer straight

**kick** (**kik**) to hit something with your foot

**knee** (**nee**) part of your body that bends in the center of the leg

**metal** (**met**-uhl) a hard material that comes from the ground and can be used to make many things, such as pots, coins, parts of cars, and jewelry

**muscles** (**muhs**-uhlz) parts of your body that stretch and make other parts of your body move

**plastic** (**plass**-tik) a material that is strong and light and does not break easily

**wheelchairs** (**weel**-chairz) chairs that move on wheels that are used by people who are not able to walk well

# To Find Out More

**Books**
*Arms and Legs and Other Limbs*
by Allan Fowler
Grolier Publishing Co., Inc.

*Legs and Feet*
by Elizabeth Miles
Heinemann Library

**Web Site**
**Kids Running**
http://www.kidsrunning.com
On this Web site, read about running for fun and
for exercise. You can also see what other kids
think about running.

# Index

About the Author

Lloyd G. Douglas has written many books for children.

Reading Consultants

Kris Flynn, Coordinator, Small School District Literacy, The San Diego County Office of Education

Shelly Forys, Certified Reading Recovery Specialist, W.J. Zahnow Elementary School, Waterloo, IL

Paulette Mansell, Certified Reading Recovery Specialist, and Early Literacy Consultant, TX